SAM COSTA'S HANDY HINTS

**587 listeners' hints from Sam Costa's
Radio-2 programme**

British Broadcasting Corporation

Published by the British Broadcasting Corporation
35 Marylebone High Street, London W1M 4AA
SBN 563 09282 3
© British Broadcasting Corporation 1970
First published 1970

Printed in England
by Hazell Watson & Viney Ltd
Aylesbury, Bucks

Contents

Foreword

Much as I should like to, I cannot take any credit for this book of hints, because they were all sent to me by the ladies, and some of the gentlemen too, who listen to my programme. No pressure was brought to bear – there was no bribery and no prizes either – not even free trading stamps! Now you know why they call me 'Sam the Skinflint'. But it was entirely due to you that this book came into being, and I thank you all most sincerely for your wonderful co-operation.

When the programme first began, in 1968, a certain producer who shall be nameless – for his own sake, as various instalment-men are trying to track him down, and have been for the past twenty years: boy, that was a mouthful! anyway, this producer suggested some 'listener participation'. I said, 'What a great idea! What does it mean?' And he explained that I should ask listeners for poems on what they were doing at home while listening to the programme. I said, 'But no one has got the time to write poems, I don't suppose I shall get four!' Well, I shall admit quite freely (now that they have removed the handcuffs and leg-irons) that I was wrong! And within a few weeks I had received more than 800 poems, and all from housewives who had never written a line of poetry in their lives before. And as that wonderful comic Frankie Howerd would say – 'I was amazed!' And I really was.

Eventually, the poems stopped coming and the Hint idea came to me, and you all started sending your own pet ones in by the hundred. In fact I was head over heels in hints, but I had treatment for it, and now I'm the right way up again. It's much more comfortable! But the hints kept on coming, and they haven't stopped yet. My wife tried many of them, and found they were most practical; it was her idea to put them into book form, which, as you see, has been done. Nevertheless, you are the people who are really responsible for it, so I thank you for all your valuable help. Hollywood has already been after the film rights, but as they wanted to make it into a movie, I had to turn down their offer. After all, what is two or three million dollars between friends? And after I had paid the tax, I should have been losing on the deal, so there will be no movie, thank heaven.

I hope the hints you will find in the book will be useful to you, and that there will be a place for it in your kitchen or, if you are very rich, in your library. By the way, the BBC have advised me that we can't be responsible if any of the hints go wrong – and if anything blows up, don't call us – and we won't call you either. By then I shall probably have fled the country! Incidentally we were going to cover the book with real sable skin, but decided that it might be a bit flashy, so we spun a coin – heads for paper and tails for paper – and as the coin slipped through the floorboards we made it paper, and sent a St Bernard to try to find the coin. I should like to close this foreword to the book with a saying that has helped me through many a dark day, when we hadn't paid the electricity bill or the gas bill and we were out of candles, which I hope will help you too. It's just this: 'You are never really poor until you have to have water on your cornflakes,' – and I hope you never do – they go all soggy. PS. All the things I have said about the BBC canteen are untrue! And I am not saying that because the restaurant manageress is a lady wrestler in her spare time. The coffee really does taste like coffee, and so does the tea, and the cocoa. PPS. Thanks for buying the book – now I can buy my wife, Esther, a new carpet for my side of the bedroom!

SAM COSTA

Food and cooking

Eggs

1 *Boiled*
When boiling eggs for the family, each with different tastes, mark the eggs with H for hardboiled, S for soft.

2
When serving boiled eggs for a hurried breakfast, cover the plates with a square of kitchen paper towelling. Shell and drips of egg can then be easily disposed of, thus making washing-up much easier.

3
After hard-boiling eggs, plunge them into cold water until needed. This will prevent the yolks from discolouring.

4
In a hard-water area, add a few drops of vinegar to the water when boiling eggs – this prevents the pan from going black.

5
Prick the rounded end of an egg with a needle to release air from the air pocket before boiling. This will prevent the egg from breaking or cracking.

6
To prevent the shell cracking while boiling, place the egg in cold water, bring to the boil, take off the heat and leave to stand for 3 to 4 minutes for soft-boiled eggs and 4 to 5 minutes for hard-boiled eggs.

7 *Scrambled*
Mix half a teaspoonful of cornflour per egg with a little milk for a better consistency.

8
Melt dripping, instead of butter, in the pan before scrambling eggs, the pan will be easier to clean.

9 *Poached*
Place a metal pastry cutter in the pan of water and break the

egg into this. The poached egg will have a fluted edge and the pan will remain clean – especially if a teaspoonful of vinegar is added to the water.

10
A dessertspoonful of milk, added to the water for poaching eggs, will prevent them sticking to the pan.

11 *Fried*
To stop fried eggs sticking to the pan, sprinkle a little salt over the base of the dry pan. Stand this over a low heat until just warm, shake out the salt, add fat, and fry the eggs in the usual way.

12 *In mashed potato*
Add a raw egg when mashing potatoes – a good way of serving eggs to children who don't like them.

13 *Separating yolks*
To separate the yolk from the white, break the egg onto a saucer, cover the yolk with half the shell and pour off the white.

14 *Cracked*
To ease out a cracked egg stuck in a carton, soak the carton in water. The egg can then be removed easily.

15 *Eggshell*
A piece of shell in egg-white can be quickly removed if you wet the spoon first.

16 *Curdling*
Risk of curdling will be greatly reduced if eggs are placed very briefly in a bowl of hot water before adding to fat and sugar – but be careful not to cook the eggs.

17 *Economy measure*
One egg and a tablespoonful of vinegar are equivalent to two eggs in a recipe.

Vegetables and fruit
18 *Potatoes*
Potatoes are easier to scrape if you put them in a colander,

swill them under a running tap, then stand the colander in a
bowl of water and add a good dessertspoonful of salt. Leave to
stand and then scrape.

19
If you peel potatoes after onions, the onion smell disappears
from the knife and hands.

20
Peel potatoes from top to bottom and they will not break when
cooking. Use a plastic pan scrubber for scraping new potatoes.

21
Peeled potatoes can be left overnight in water to which a little
milk has been added and they will not discolour. Swill before
boiling.

22
Scrape new potatoes the night before use and leave standing in
unsalted cold water. Then plunge them into boiling salted
water to cook. This will improve flavour and cut down boiling
time.

23
After peeling green or dark potatoes, stand them in water and
add a piece of scrubbed coal; the potatoes will turn white.

24
Potatoes will not turn green if they are removed from their
polythene bag and stored in a dark place.

25
Add a squeeze of lemon juice to new potatoes before cooking,
to keep them white.

26
Add a knob of margarine or butter, or a little vinegar, to the
water while boiling potatoes and they will not boil over.

27
When mashing potatoes, mix in half a teaspoonful of baking
powder. This makes them light and fluffy.

28
Cook old potatoes in cold water, and new ones in hot.

29

Before cooking baked potatoes, soak them for fifteen minutes in very hot water. They will cook in half the time and taste delicious.

30 *Chips*

Soak chipped potatoes in water before frying to remove some of the starch and prevent them sticking together during cooking. Dry them well, then plunge them into hot fat.

31

After cutting chips for frying, pop them into boiling salted water for 4 to 5 minutes, drain well (any surplus moisture will quickly evaporate) then fry as usual.

32 *Onions*

After peeling onions, rub a little mustard into your hands to remove the smell.

33

If a small amount of onion is all that is needed, just slice off as much as is necessary – no need to peel – then wrap the rest in tin foil. It keeps very well.

34

To avoid tears when peeling onions, first soak them in water to soften the skin. Then cut off the top and peel down to the root; cut the root off last.

35

Or peel the onions under water.

36

Onions are more tasty and less greasy if they are parboiled, then drained, before frying. It is simpler to then fry them in a chip basket.

37 *Cauliflower*

To keep cauliflower white, put a tablespoonful of milk into the water, when cooking.

38

Place a crust of bread on top of a cauliflower when cooking – it absorbs most of the smell.

39 Greens
Put a pinch of bicarbonate soda in the greens' water and they will keep their colour. This also helps soften greens that look stringy or tough.

40 Cabbage
A teaspoonful of lemon juice, added to cabbage water, will reduce the smell.

41
The *tiniest* piece of soda, added to cabbage water, reduces the cooking smell and also makes it very tender.

42
Or some sugar in the water will help to diminish the smell.

43 Lids off
Vegetables grown above ground should be cooked with the lid off, those grown underground, with the lid on.

44 Salt
Do not add salt to the vegetables until the water has boiled; this saves the pan from becoming pitted.

45 Straining
To strain vegetables, cover them with a lid smaller than the pan they are in. This holds them secure while the water is poured off.

46 Runner beans
Use a potato peeler to string runner beans.

47 Mushrooms
Mushrooms plunged into boiling water for a minute or so before frying or grilling will be more succulent and will not shrivel.

48 Lettuce
A imp lettuce. put in cold water with a lump of clean coal added, soon revives.

49
To keep lettuce fresh and crisp. soak it in water with fresh lemon juice.

If you haven't a fridge, keep lettuce fresh by washing it, then storing it in a closed saucepan.

51 *Celery*
Celery will stay crisper if stood in cold water with a little sugar added (one teaspoonful to a quart of water).

52 *Radishes*
When serving radishes for salads, split the root end several times towards the stalk end, place in a bowl of water, and the radishes will open like flowers.

53 *Parsley*
To keep parsley fresh, rinse it in cold water, drain, then store it in an airtight bottle or plastic bag, in the lower part of the fridge.

54 *Lemons*
Lemons can be preserved by smearing them completely with the white or yolk of an egg. Place singly on a shelf to dry. Treated in this way they will keep for a long time, even in hot weather.

55
Or place lemons in a jar of water, and change the water every day or two. This will keep them fresh for several weeks.

56
Or lemons will keep fresh if covered with buttermilk or sour milk, which should be changed each week.

57
Cut lemons will keep fresh if placed on a saucer and covered with an upturned tumbler.

58
A teaspoonful of lemon or orange juice added to cake mixture helps the cake rise and makes it lighter in texture.

59
If only a few drops of lemon are required, pierce the lemon skin with a knitting needle instead of cutting it in half.

60 *Apples*
Save old nylons, place an apple at the toe, tie a knot, then place another sound apple above the knot and so on. Hang them in a cold dry place, and cut them off from the bottom as required.

61
To avoid discoloured apples, peel them under water.

62
When preparing apples for baking, cut the skin horizontally round the apple. This prevents them from turning mushy.

63
Steep apples in salt water to keep them white – they will keep for hours.

64 *Rhubarb*
Cut rhubarb with a pair of sharp scissors, not a knife. This is much quicker, and doesn't skin the fruit.

65
Half a teaspoonful of seed tapioca, added to the water when cooking rhubarb, plums, etc., makes a thick juice.

66 *Cooking pears*
Peel, quarter and core the pears, drop them in salted water, swill and drain them, put them in a pan, cover with a flagon of clear, fizzy lemonade, add a little sugar and stew until tender.

Jam
67 *Whole fruit*
When making whole fruit jam, allow it to cool for five minutes, then stir before potting. The fruit will then settle evenly.

68 *Damson*
Do not stir damson jam once it has been boiled, or the damsons will shred.

69 *Tasting*
When tasting jam or jelly in hot weather, cool the 'test' jam rapidly in the lower part of the fridge for a few moments, this saves the risk of over-boiling.

70 *Jam-pot covers*
To make airtight jam-pots covers for home-made jam: cut

rounds of greaseproof, larger than the top of the jar, dip these into hot starch, cover the pots immediately and seal with an elastic band. The covers will dry like parchment.

71 *Jam pans*
When making jam, first grease the bottom of the pan, the jam will not burn or stick and washing-up is made much easier.

72 *Drupe fruits (plums, greengages, etc.)*
1 Buy several pounds of the fruit, or one pound of each.
2 Wash and de-stalk it, then separate it into ripe for eating, and under- and over-ripe for dessert and jam.
3 Place the under- and over-ripe fruit in a large saucepan, cover with water and boil for 5 to 10 minutes.
4 Strain, then separate the whole fruit from the pulp. Use the whole fruit in a pie, adding the necessary sugar, or simply place it in an oven-proof dish, cover with sugar, add lid and gently heat in oven for 20 minutes.
5 Discard the stones from the pulp, then reheat it in a saucepan. Add sugar gradually until the mixture thickens, then boil. A squirt of lemon juice will help to set the jam. Leave to cool, then transfer to jars. Eat within a week, unless preserving, in sterilised, air-free containers.

73 *Jelly*
After making jam or marmalade, do not wash the pan immediately but put in half a pint of water and half a jelly, then bring it to melting point, stirring well. This makes a good fruity-flavoured jelly.

74 *Fruit jars*
Fruit jars that are hard to open should be stood upside down in hot (not boiling) water for a few minutes. They will then open easily.

75 *Bottled Fruit*
When opening a jar of bottled fruit for pie making, pour off the surplus liquid into a saucepan, add two tablespoonfuls of sugar and boil for a few minutes. If this is added to a lb jar of jam, it will double the quantity and make a good filling for jam tarts.

Puddings and pies

76 *Bread and butter pudding*
Spice bread and butter pudding, by putting layers of thinly sliced apples between the bread and the currants.

77 *Fruit pies*
When baking a fruit or meat pie, stand the dish within a larger dish containing a little water. This will prevent juice or gravy spilling over into the oven.

78 *Steamed pudding*
If a steamer is unavailable, cover a steamed pudding with a cloth and secure with a length of string or material, leaving enough to tie loosely across the top of the pudding to make a handle to lower in and out of the saucepan.

79 *Yorkshire pudding*
To make a perfect Yorkshire pudding, you must have your fat really hot so that as you pour the mixture in, it immediately begins to cook.

80
Try adding some dried sage and a little finely grated onion to Yorkshire pudding.

81 *Cottage pie*
When making cottage pie, add some baked beans.

82 *Pancakes*
A listener assures us that vinegar and sugar on pancakes is delicious.

83 *Christmas pudding and cake*
When mixing Christmas pudding or cake, add a tablespoonful of bicarbonate of soda mixed with a teaspoonful of vinegar. This makes the mixture darker when cooked. Also add 4 ozs of shelled and chopped walnuts, 2 tablespoonfuls of cocoa and 1 tablespoonful of coffee essence, to the cake.

84
Leftover Christmas pudding is delicious fried, or sprinkled with brown sugar and lightly grilled.

85 *Apple pie*
When preparing an apple pie, add a little grated lemon peel.

Cakes and biscuits
86 *Christmas cake frills*
Instead of putting the conventional frill round the Christmas cake and laboriously undoing it each time the cake is cut, arrange paper doilies cut in half, one end tucked under the cake, round the edge. Then just remove one doily for each slice.

87 *Decorations*
Attractive finishes to iced cakes can be made by covering the backs of rose or holly leaves (but not ivy leaves as they are poisonous!) with icing or chocolate, and arranging these on the cake.

88 *Butter cream*
Any leftover butter cream can be used up between rich tea biscuits.

89 *Icing*
Small rosettes, made from leftover royal icing, will keep for weeks in an airtight tin.

90 *Chocolate buttons*
Instead of melting chocolate to ice small cakes, place a few chocolate buttons on top of each cake and put them in a hot oven for a minute or two.

91 *Meringues*
When making meringues, or royal icing, always scald the utensils to be used, as any grease on them will prevent egg whites from stiffening.

92 *Sour cream*
A pinch of bicarbonate of soda will stop whipped fresh cream from turning sour in cakes. It will also take the bitterness from sour cream which may then be flavoured and used as cake filling.

93 *Cocoa*
When using cocoa powder in cakes, mix it with a little milk and add it when beating in the eggs.

94 *Iced cake*
A simple way of putting iced cakes into tins: stand the cake on the lid and place the tin over it, then store the tin upside down.

95 *Fresh cake*
Put a small sound apple in the cake tin with a fruit cake and it will keep the cake moist.

96
To freshen stale cake, put it in a covered basin and steam for about half an hour.

97 *Fruit cake*
If you have any marmalade that has fermented, add it to your next spiced fruit cake for a delicious flavour.

98 *Sponge cake*
To prevent sponge cakes sticking, grease and flour the tins before putting in the mixture. When cooked, turn them onto a damp cloth at once and when cool, turn onto a wire tray.

99 *Lining tins*
Wax paper from cereal packets is excellent for lining cake tins – no greasing necessary.

100
Line your biscuit tin with blotting paper, it will absorb the moisture and keep the biscuits crisp.

101 *Biscuit crumbs*
Put biscuit crumbs into a polythene bag, crush them finely with a rolling pin and use for decorating desserts.

Bread
102
To freshen a stale loaf of bread, dampen the sides with water and place in a warm oven for 10 to 15 minutes, or until crisp.

103
Or place bread or scones, without dampening, in the top of a double boiler. Bring to the boil, then simmer for a few minutes.

104

Bread can be kept fresh for several days if stored in the bottom part of a refrigerator.

105

Don't throw away the polythene bags from packets of grease-proof paper. Bread keeps fresher if first wrapped in grease-proof, then in the polythene bag, and secured with a rubber band.

106

When cutting a fresh loaf, use a hot knife to prevent it crumbling.

107

Some grains of rice kept in the bread bin, will keep bread moist and fresh much longer.

108 *Breadcrumbs*

If breadcrumbs are unavailable, crush a packet of crisps or cornflakes and use these for frying.

109

An easy way of making white breadcrumbs is to rub the bread through a colander.

110 *Toast*

To prevent toast curling at the edges, put a little water in the grill pan.

Pastry

111

On baking day make the pastry first. If it is made to the correct consistency, the bowl should be clean enough to use for cake-making.

112

Rubbing the fat down a grater saves kneading time.

113

Try making pastry with an egg instead of water; it will be soft and melting and a nice gold colour after baking.

114

Put a dessertspoonful of semolina in with the flour. It makes crisp pastry.

115
Make pastry with vinegar instead of water – it gives it a light and crumbly texture.

116
When picking up pastry to cover a pie, place the rolling pin on the edge of the pastry and roll up loosely, put rolling pin with pastry in position over the pie and unroll.

117
Always put a narrow edge of pastry round the edge of a pie before putting the pastry on top. This will prevent the pastry from shrinking. It also makes trimming the pastry edge easier.

118
Use an apple corer with a fluted edge for trimming pastry edges.

119
When reheating pastry cover with a greaseproof paper or foil to prevent burning.

120
Make suet pastry for steamed steak and kidney pudding with plain, not self-raising, flour and you will find that the gravy will stay within the crust and not seep through.

121
Do not roll the trimmings of flaky pastry into a ball, but lay the pieces on top of one another, then roll out. This way the flakiness is not impaired.

Fish
122 *Fishy smells*
To prepare fish for fish pie or fish cakes without dreadful smells, first skin the fish, bring a saucepan of water to the boil, put in the fish and put the lid on. Turn off the gas, leave to stand for about 15 to 30 minutes according to the amount of fish. Drain off the water, or use for sauce. The fish will flake easily.

123
Kippers too can be cooked without a smell: pierce their tails with a skewer, suspend them in a jug, pour on boiling water and leave for about five minutes.

124 *Fishy dishes*
When washing-up, rinse fish dishes under the cold tap first. This will prevent a fishy smell in the washing-up water.

125 *Fried fish*
If you are short of an egg when frying fish, put some custard powder on a plate, mix with a little water, dip the fish in, then into bread crumbs and fry as usual.

126
Save flour-bags which are almost empty. When you need to coat fish with flour, drop one piece in the bag at a time and shake it.

127
When frying fish in batter, add a little vinegar to the hot fat before cooking. This gives the batter extra flavour and keeps it crisp.

128 *Tuna fish*
Try the vinegar from pickled onions with tuna fish.

Meats
129 *Sausages*
Before cooking 'bangers', coat them in a little flour. This will stop the skins from splitting and they will cook a golden brown.

130
To prevent sausages from splitting and shrivelling, first put them into boiling water for a minute, dry them, then fry in the usual way.

131
Skinned sausages make excellent sausage-meat for Scotch eggs.

132 *Liver*
Before cooking liver, dip each piece in milk, then flour. This seals in the juices and makes it tender.

133
When cooking liver, first plunge it into boiling water before cooking and it will always be tender.

134 *Bacon*
Before cooking bacon, cut four half-inch slits in the fat. The rashers will stay flat and fry evenly.

135 *Poultry*
Never throw a poultry carcass away. Boiled up, it makes excellent stock.

136
After stuffing a chicken or turkey, completely cover the opening with greaseproof paper. Then cook in the usual way, but be sure to remove the paper before carving.

137
If you plunge poultry into boiling water it will be much easier to pluck.

138
Frozen chicken, soaked in salt water overnight, regains lost flavour.

139 *Casseroles*
Stand a casserole dish on a large heat-proof plate or tin in the oven. This collects any gravy that might spill over, and makes it easier to remove the casserole from the oven.

140 *Roast meat*
The Sunday joint can be kept moist if placed in a saucepan, or basin, and covered with hot gravy.

141 *Dripping*
When saving fat from roast meat, put a tablespoonful of water in the bottom of the basin before pouring in the fat; any sediment will collect in this and can be discarded.

Soups and stews
142
To remove fat from the top of hot soups and stews, lay a piece of absorbent paper over the top.

Hot dinners
143
To keep a late arrival's dinner hot, place the plate, covered with a lid, over a saucepan of hot water.

144
A meal can be kept hot in the oven without becoming dry, if a bowl of water is placed alongside it.

145

Save butter and margarine wrappings to cover meat meals left in the oven.

Cheese

146 *Welsh rarebit*

Grate or thinly flake some cheese into a breakfast cup until it is three parts full. Pour on boiling water and leave to stand for ten minutes. Pour off the water and the cheese will be like a thick cream at the bottom. Serve on hot toast with salt and pepper to taste.

147

A piece of tin foil, lining the bottom of the grill pan, saves cleaning when cooking welsh rarebit.

148 *Grated cheese*

Grate dry stale cheese and store it in an airtight container. Use for cheese sauce or any dishes requiring grated cheese.

149 *Mouldy cheese*

To prevent mould place a lump of sugar in the cheese dish.

Milk

150

To prevent milk boiling over, place an ordinary pie chimney in the centre of the saucepan. The milk will boil up through the chimney and not over the edge.

151

After boiling milk in a saucepan, wipe the pan with a damp cloth while it is still hot. It will come absolutely clean without water.

152

Milk is less likely to burn if the saucepan is first rinsed in cold water.

153

When taking the cream or a little milk from the bottle, pour over the back of a dessertspoon, to prevent splashing or dripping.

Custard

154
When making custard, use demerara sugar and no skin will form.

155
After making custard, sprinkle it with sugar and cover immediately with a saucer or plate and there will be no skin.

156
If custard or gravy becomes lumpy, allow it to cool, then whisk it with a rotary beater. The lumps will disappear and it can then be reheated.

Glass casserole dishes

157
Use butter and margarine papers to grease glass casserole dishes and baking tins; pay special attention to the edges and corners. This makes washing up much easier and does away with brown marks on glassware.

Butter

158
To use butter taken straight from the fridge, cut it into small pieces then mash it with a fork warmed in hot water.

Rice

159
To prevent rice or spaghetti from boiling over, add a knob of margarine or a tablespoonful of oil to the water.

Sandwiches

160 *Meat*
Meat sandwiches are much tastier if first spread with dripping.

161
Cut luncheon meat for sandwiches by opening the tin at both ends, push the meat out gently, then slice off close to the tin. You'll get whole slices and no crumbs.

162 *Chocolate and banana*
Try a sandwich filling of chocolate spread and bananas.

Seasonings, spices and sauces

163 *Salt*

A pinch of salt:

stops the white running out of an egg which cracks while boiling

adds flavour when percolating coffee

makes egg white go further when making meringues

removes burn marks from saucepans if left to soak for a short while.

164

A little salt added to mustard will keep it moist for a long time.

165

A few grains of rice in the salt cellar will prevent the salt becoming damp.

166 *Mustard*

Keep made mustard in a screw-top jar to prevent it from drying up.

167 *Mint Sauce*

When chopping mint for mint sauce, first sprinkle it with sugar and it will chop in half the time.

168

Add a little grated onion when making mint sauce.

169 *Mayonnaise*

When making mayonnaise, add one dessertspoonful of boiling water to the dry ingredients, mix well, then add the vinegar and oil. The mayonnaise will not curdle.

170 *White sauce*

When making a white sauce from flour, mix a little granulated sugar with the dry flour for a smooth sauce.

171 *Apple sauce*

Apple purée, sold as baby food, makes tasty apple sauce to go with pork.

Almonds

172

Before putting blanched almonds on top of a fruit cake, soak them in milk for a minute, then wipe them dry. They will not burn or go brown while cooking.

Sugar

173

Castor or icing sugar can be made from granulated sugar in a liquidiser.

174

If your brown sugar becomes lumpy, put it in the bread-bin and the lumps disappear.

175

Should brown sugar harden in its container, add half an apple and this will soften it.

Tea

176

If you do not possess an automatic tea-maker, make the tea the night before and keep it in a vacuum flask on your bedside table ready for the morning.

Sundry cooking hints

177 *Hot lids*

Use a spring-clip clothes peg for removing hot lids from pans when they have only small knobs or handles.

178 *Boiled kettles*

To refill a kettle after it has boiled, run water in through the spout, then the lid can be removed without fear of scalding.

179 *Sauce bottles*

To empty the last drains of a sauce bottle, immerse the bottle in hot water for a minute.

180 *Clean fingers*

A crust of bread, dipped in vinegar, can be used to remove fruit and vegetable stains from the fingers.

181 *Cooking smells*

Cooking smells will be reduced if a damp newspaper is placed on the plate rack above the cooker.

182 *Graters*

Clean orange or lemon peel from your grater with a pastry brush.

Handy measures
183

	One level breakfast cup equals:	One level tablespoonful equals:
Fresh breadcrumbs	3 ozs	$\frac{1}{4}$ oz
Fine dried breadcrumbs	6 ozs	$\frac{1}{3}$ oz
Grated cheese	4 ozs	$\frac{1}{4}$ oz
Cocoa powder ⎫ Cornflour ⎬ Custard powder ⎭	5 ozs	$\frac{1}{4}$ oz
Flour	6 ozs	$\frac{1}{3}$ oz
Golden syrup	1 lb	1 oz
Jam	12 ozs	1 oz
Lard, margarine or butter	9 ozs	1 oz
Raisins	$6\frac{1}{2}$ ozs	$\frac{1}{2}$ oz
Semolina	9 ozs	$\frac{1}{2}$ oz
Granulated sugar	10 ozs	$\frac{1}{2}$ oz
Sultanas	7 ozs	$\frac{1}{2}$ oz

Cleaning and washing

Sticky marks
184
To remove unsightly marks, left by stick-on price labels, from plastic, china, or enamelware, rub on a little wax furniture polish or nail-varnish remover.

Fireplaces
185
To remove marks from fireplaces, dip a damp scrubbing brush into the fire ash and then rub the marks, which will soon disappear. Wipe clean with a damp cloth.

Furniture
186 *Scratches*
Rub a broken piece of walnut, or half a brazil nut, across a scratched polished surface, then polish with a soft cloth. Camphorated oil, rubbed well into furniture with the tip of the finger, will remove any superficial scratches.

187 *Heat marks*
To remove heat marks on a polished surface, collect a teaspoonful of cigarette ash, dip a moistened cloth into it, and rub this on the heat mark. This also works on spirit stains.

188
A similar method is to rub the heat stain with a soft cloth that has been dipped in spirit of camphor. Rub with a circular motion until the stain has disappeared, then polish with furniture wax.

189
A carpenter advised rubbing a little metal polish on a soft cloth over the mark.

190
Rub methylated spirits into the mark, then some *raw* linseed oil and when the offending mark has disappeared, polish with a good furniture wax.

191 *Ink spots*

Ink spots can be removed from wooden furniture quite safely by using a solution comprising equal parts of vinegar and linseed oil.

192 *Extra shine*

To give polished wood an extra shine, make up a solution of half a cup of vinegar to a gallon of water. Wring out a soft cloth in this solution, rub down the furniture, then polish with a soft duster.

193 *Upholstered furniture*

Cover a rolling pin with sticky tape – wound sticky side outwards – and roll it over your furniture. Animal fur and pieces of wool or cotton will adhere to it.

Stained fingers

194

To prevent getting a stained thumb while scraping or peeling potatoes, use a rubber thimble – the sort bank clerks use for counting notes.

195

Cut off any good fingers from old rubber gloves and use these as finger shields when peeling potatoes.

196

When scraping new potatoes, try adding salt or vinegar to the water; this will keep your hands clean.

Rubber gloves

197

Rubber gloves can be reinforced if they are turned inside out and small pieces of elastoplast stuck over each finger tip.

198

Inexpensive talcum power kept by the sink and sprinkled into rubber gloves makes them easier to pull on and off.

Soap

199

To join two thin pieces of soap together, soften both in hot water for a few seconds, then push the thinner of the two onto the other, as if applying a patch to a rubber tube.

200

A new bar of soap can be made by saving all the small pieces and melting them down in an old basin over a saucepan of boiling water. When they have all melted, allow to cool and then mould into a new bar.

201

Put the soap pieces into a jelly mould, pour on boiling water and when cool, cover and put into the fridge.

202

Save all scraps of soap in a plastic bag with small holes in (the sort that potatoes or lettuce come in) and keep for bath nights. Children love to squeeze the bag and make soapy bubbles.

203

Soap kept on a piece of foam rubber will prevent the soap going soggy and makes a good soapy pad for cleaning wash basins etc.

Stains

204 *Grass stains*

Rub methylated spirit, before washing, into grass stains on clothes, especially cricket whites.

205 *Mould stains*

Mould and rust stains can be removed from clothes or carpets made of natural fibres by rubbing gently with a piece of cotton wool dipped in oxalic acid.

206 *Grease spots*

To remove a grease spot from upholstery, simply rub cornmeal into it, then vacuum clean the next day.

207 *Paint stains*

If you should accidentally get paint onto clothes, rub the spot with a similar piece of fabric. The paint, being sticky when fresh, will roll off without any cleanser.

208 *Tar stains*

If you are unlucky enough to get tar on your clothes from the beach, sponge gently with cotton wool soaked in oil of eucalyptus and it will soon disappear.

209 *White clothes*

To remove a stain from a white garment, mix a little whitening to a paste with some milk, rub this onto the stain, leave to dry, then brush the area well.

210 *Grease marks*

To remove a grease mark, place blotting paper over and under the mark and iron with a hot iron. The paper should absorb the grease.

211 *Oil stains*

To remove oil from clothing pour a drop of eucalyptus oil straight from the bottle onto the spot. Then wash the garment in the usual way.

Rinsing dishes
212

After washing-up, rinse the articles in hot water and leave to drain dry. Even the cleanest teacloths can harbour germs, especially in hot weather, which can lead to food poisoning.

Broken eggs
213

To clean broken egg off the floor, sprinkle the area with salt, leave for 20 to 30 minutes and then sweep up.

Old toothbrushes
214

Save old toothbrushes; they are very useful for cleaning in awkward places, polishing silver and cleaning ashtrays.

Sweeping
215

To keep dust from flying around when sweeping, dampen both the broom bristles and the inside of the dustpan.

216

To seal a garage or cement floor, which gives off clouds of dust when swept, make up a solution of waterglass, used for egg preserving, brush on after sweeping and allow to dry.

217
Before sweeping dusty paths, or garages, sprinkle the ground with used damp tea leaves; this will stop the dust rising.

Flower vases
218
To remove green mould from the bottom of narrow-necked flower vases, put in a teaspoonful of uncooked rice and a little water. Shake, rinse well, and you will have a sparkling base.

Narrow-necked bottles
219
Narrow-necked bottles can be cleaned by putting crushed egg-shell and *warm* water in the bottle, shaking well and then rinsing.

Glassware
220
If glassware becomes stained and cannot be cleaned by ordinary washing, try adding a large spoonful of sugar to the water.

Glasses and cups
221
To clean the inside of a wine glass or spirit decanter, fill the decanter with water, drop in one or two denture cleaning tablets and leave overnight. Metal teapots and plastic cups and mugs can also be cleaned by this method.

222
Stained teacups can be cleaned with salt and water.

Metals
223 *Silverware*
If your cutlery is discoloured, crush a sheet of silver paper (or some milk bottle tops) and add it, together with a teaspoonful of salt, to a glass of water. Then place your spoons and forks in this for a few minutes.

224 *Chrome*
To keep a chrome kettle or coffee pot looking bright and shiny, dip a damp cloth in bicarbonate of soda, rub this over the chrome and leave to dry. Then polish with a soft cloth.

225 *Brass*
For outdoor brass, such as key locks, letterboxes and knockers, choose a dry day, polish brass as usual until gleaming, then give it a **quick** thin coat of colourless nail polish. On the wettest and dampest day, the brass will remain shining. Repeat the treatment in about a year, first cleaning with nail polish remover.

226
The best way to remove tarnish from brass is to dip a cloth into a solution of salt and vinegar and rub the brass, then polish in the normal way.

227 *Brass rings*
Brass curtain hooks and rings can be cleaned by placing in a solution of vinegar and water.

228 *Copper*
Clean copper with half a lemon dipped in some salt.

White tiles
229
Use liquid shoe whitener, or white window cream, to clean tiles; it polishes the tiles and makes the grouting white.

Ash trays
230
After cleaning ash trays, smear a little polish inside. This will make cleaning much easier next time, since the ash will not stick.

Jewellery
231
Put jewellery into a small container, cover with methylated spirits, then gently shake this. Remove after about five minutes. The dirt will have come out, the spirit will evaporate and with a gentle rub on a chamois leather the jewels will be sparkling.

232
Soak rings in gin to clean them.

Skirting boards

233

To prevent chipped skirting boards while vacuum cleaning, stick some self-adhesive foam draught-excluder round the bottom edge of the cleaner.

Suds

234

If detergent suds will not disappear, waggle a piece of soap in them and they will dissipate like magic.

Wallpaper

235

Marks on wallpaper can be removed by soaking a cloth in paraffin and leaving to dry. When it is completely dry, rub the wallpaper with it and it should come clean and fresh.

Oily hands

236

Wash oily or greasy hands in neat washing-up liquid. Rub it in well, then rinse in cold water (hot water opens the pores and lets the dirt sink in).

Doorsteps

237

To keep doorsteps free from ice, add a cupful of methylated spirits to a pail of water and wash the steps with this solution.

Blackened ceilings

238

Wash the black patches with a fairly thick mixture of cold water starch. Leave to dry thoroughly, then rub with a soft duster.

Bottle labels

239

Bottles with paper labels giving instructions for use can be kept clean by covering with sellotape.

Camphor

240

Place a piece of camphor inside a tool box, or trinket box, to prevent rusting or tarnishing.

Shoes

241 *Sea-stained*

Shoes marked by sea water can be cleaned by brushing off the dirt, then rubbing the white stain with half a lemon. Leave overnight, brush, and then polish in the usual way.

242 *Discoloured*

To restore discoloured shoes, lather the uppers with a lather shaving cream; leave for about fifteen minutes, then wipe off with a clean towel. Allow to dry slowly, then clean in the usual way.

243 *Cleaning shoes*

When cleaning shoes, especially sandals, keep a polythene bag over your hand to prevent it becoming stained by the polish.

Watch-faces

244

To remove scratches from the face of a wrist or pocket watch, polish with a little liquid brass polish.

Sticky tape

245

A roll of sticky tape, carried in the handbag, makes an excellent emergency clothes brush – the sticky side picks up fluff and loose threads from clothing.

Animal hairs

246

Animal hairs can be removed from furniture with a piece of foam rubber.

Brushing clothes

247

When brushing clothes, dip the tips of the bristles of the brush in water, this helps to pick up specks more easily.

Windows and mirrors

248 *Eau-de-Cologne*

Windows and mirrors can be cleaned with a few drops of eau-de-Cologne on a soft cloth. This removes greasy marks and deters flies and mosquitoes.

249 *Glycerine*
Rub a little glycerine or washing-up liquid onto the window panes, then buff them off with a soft cloth. This stops them steaming up.

250 *Methylated spirits*
To remove hair lacquer from mirrors, or any polished surface, sprinkle methylated spirits onto a soft cloth and wipe gently, then polish with a dry soft duster. This is also an excellent way of cleaning windows.

251 *Long broom*
A nylon sweeping broom, dipped in a bucket of hot soapy water, makes easy work of dirty windows for those who do not have step ladders or who cannot climb them.

252 *Newspaper*
To get an extra polish on windows, brass or copper, use a well screwed-up newspaper.

Saucepans
253
A saucepan, badly burnt inside, can be cleaned by filling it with water, then adding a sliced onion and a desertspoonful of salt. Leave to soak overnight and the burnt food will wash away easily.

254
Add hot water to a burnt pan, together with a teaspoonful of cream of tartar for each quart of water used. Simmer for twenty minutes, allow to cool slowly, then wipe clean.

255
Clean empty milk or potato saucepans in cold water as soon as possible after use.

256
Wipe a milk saucepan with a damp cloth immediately after use.

Stainless steel pots
257
Stainless steel teapots can be cleaned inside by adding a table-spoonful of detergent powder, pouring on boiling water, leaving to soak, then rinsing well.

258
Alternatively, fill the teapot with Milton solution, one table-spoonful to two pints of water, leave it to soak for a while, then rinse well.

Vacuum flasks
259
To clean a vacuum flask, put half a teaspoonful of bicarbonate of soda in the flask and fill with boiling water. Leave to stand overnight, then rinse well.

Cleaning ovens
260
After using the oven, leave the door ajar. This enables the steam to escape, instead of condensing on the inside of the oven and cuts down cleaning-time by half. (Not to be recommended if there are children or elderly people about.)

261
Place a saucerful of ammonia in the bottom of the oven as soon as it has been used. Leave the oven to cool, remove the saucer, and when you wipe down, the grease will come off easily.

262
To keep the oven clean, line it with tin foil.

263 *Hotplates*
Line underneath the hotplates of electric cookers with tinfoil, taking great care not to touch the elements. The foil can be quickly removed and makes cleaning much easier.

Baths
264
To clean and polish baths, or porcelain sinks, mix equal quantities of turpentine and linseed oil. Apply with a soft cloth. Store the mixture in an airtight bottle, away from children. Shake well before use.

265
Neat paraffin is also good for cleaning badly stained baths.

Sinks
266
Instead of sprinkling sink cleaning powder directly into the

sink, sprinkle the powder onto a cloth. This is just as effective and twice as economical.

267
Fine ash from fire grates will remove stains from sinks, baths and tiled floors.

268 *Salt for sinks*
Should you run out of sink cleaning powder use cooking salt.

Washing-up
269
When the washing-up liquid bottle appears empty, cut off the top and fill with a little water. There will be enough for four or five more wash-ups.

Empty polish tins
270
When you think that your tin of silver or brass polish is empty, open the bottom with a tin-opener and you will find enough for another polishing.

Polishing lino
271
Mix a tablespoonful of paraffin with a pint of lukewarm water, apply this to lino with a soft cloth and leave to dry. This leaves your lino shiny, but not slippery.

Sheepskin rugs
272
Sheepskin rugs can be cleansed by sprinkling them with powdered chalk, then rubbing them with a damp cloth. Repeat this three times, and then shampoo lightly and allow to dry.

273
Wash short-haired sheepskin rugs in soapy water, then rinse well and either spin dry or hang on the line. Brush well when dry or, better still, leave hanging on the line and beat with a bamboo cane.

Carpets
274
To remove stains from carpets, make a thick paste of salt and

milk, apply this to the stain and leave to dry. Then brush the area well.

275
An easy way to remove dirty marks from a light-coloured carpet is to squeeze a little washing-up liquid onto a damp cloth, rub the mark well with this until it disappears, then rinse the cloth in clean water and rub over the spot again.

276
A single mark on a carpet can be removed by rubbing the mark with the milled edge of a silver coin.

277
To keep a carpet looking bright and clean, wipe it over once a week with a sponge squeezed in a solution of vinegar and ammonia in warm water.

278
Cat or dog hairs can be removed from carpets with a sharp-toothed comb. Comb in the same direction as the pile.

279
Coffee stains can be removed from carpets by using a solution of sodium bicarbonate in warm water.

Lampshades
280
Instead of dusting fine lampshades made from georgette or silk, use a hand-held hairdryer to blow the dust off. This is very quick, and will not wear or soil the shade.

Scouring pads
281
Scouring pads for saucepans can be made by folding a sheet of fine emery cloth to a handy size and using with a strong detergent solution.

Steel wool pads
282
Steel wool pads will last a long time if they are kept in a jar of water, with a lump of soda.

283
If kept in a jar with a little water and detergent, pads of steel will not rust.

Blocked sinks
284
To clear a blocked sink, pour down a handful of bicarbonate of soda followed by half a cup of vinegar; then hold the plug in firmly. This should clear any obstruction.

Overflow outlets
285
Overflow outlets of sinks and washbasins can be cleaned by filling a small polythene spray bottle with diluted bleach and spraying into the outlet.

Disinfecting nappies
286
Never throw away the cold water sterilising solution used for baby's feeding bottles. If you tip it into the pail of soaking nappies, it helps to disinfect and bleach them.

Handkerchiefs
287
Put a small bath cube into the water when boiling handkerchiefs, this gives them a pleasant perfume when dry.

Woollen socks
288
To stop woollen socks from shrinking cut a piece of card slightly larger than the sole of the foot, place one inside the foot of each sock when washed, then peg them up to dry.

289
Woollen socks sometimes harden after washing. A handful of salt in warm water with biological pre-wash powder prevents this.

Jumpers
290
Jumpers and cardigans with sagging wrists can be restored to their original shape by dipping the bottoms of the sleeves into very hot water and leaving them to dry.

Washing velvet
291
All velvet can be washed providing it is treated in the same way

as a drip-dry fabric. It can also be pressed very lightly on the wrong side to remove stubborn creases.

Wet-day washing
292
Keep the plastic covers and hangers you get from the cleaners and use them to hang drip-dry garments outside on wet days.

Nylon underwear
293
When washing nylon undies in a machine place them in a pillow case tied at the top. They can then be put into the washing machine with the other washing and will not get twisted or damaged.

294
If you have any odd nylons that are unladdered, boil them together and you will find that they all come out the same colour.

Overalls
295
After washing overalls, immerse them in a very thick solution of starch, then, when they are almost dry, iron them on the wrong side. This will stop any oil or grease penetrating through and makes the overalls much easier to wash the next time.

Detergent packets
296
A detergent packet placed inside a plastic bag can save the powder from many a spill – especially when going to the launderette.

Timing a wash
297
An egg-timer is very useful for timing a wash in a machine unequipped with modern gadgets, as four minutes is the usual time for a wash.

Washing machines
298
Should your washing machine stick and not wash clothes properly, switch it on and run some very hot water and soda through it. This should loosen the scum that clogs up the works.

Net curtains

299
After washing nylon curtains, put them up while they are still wet, if they are hung with rods top and bottom. This ensures that they dry to the right size. The rods can be pushed through easily if a small thimble is placed over one end of the rod.

300
When washing white nylon net curtains, add a blue bag to the last rinse and leave to soak until the water turns deep blue. This stops nets from going yellow.

301
A tablespoonful of sugar added to the last rinse will make nylon or terylene crisp.

302
If your net curtains are hung on expanding plastic cord wires, leave these in place when washing them. This saves time, and weights the curtains down and holds them straight while they are drying.

Blankets

303
If you wash your blankets in the spring, all the loose fluff which falls in the garden while they are drying, will be collected by the birds to line their nests.

Pegs

304
On cold wash days put pegs onto a tin plate and place them in the oven to warm. When hanging out the clothes, this helps to keep your fingers warm.

305
Peg all the clothes before going outside. This saves fishing in the peg bag every second.

Peg marks

306
Avoid peg marks on jumpers by threading a stocking through the sleeves via the neck and pegging the stocking to the line.

Clothes-line marks

307

To prevent the clothes-line mark on jumpers that is so hard to press out, peg a folded strip of cellophane on the line first.

Nappies

308

Always peg babies' nappies about two inches from the edge and you will never have ragged or torn edges.

309

Make the last rinse for babies' nappies in really hot water – they will dry in half the time and be twice as fluffy.

Stockings

310

A glass marble, dropped into the toes of stockings, will anchor them down if you are drying them on a windy day.

Dry stockings or tights by hanging them inside a nightdress or thin garment of similar length; this stops them getting snagged or tangled.

Ironing

311 *Nylon and wool*

When ironing, have a double sheet of newspaper handy and press nylon and wool under this. It saves having to wait for the iron to cool.

312 *Sheets*

You need never iron sheets if you fold them neatly, then iron other things on top of them.

313 *Handkerchiefs*

Handkerchiefs need no ironing if they are pressed flat round the inside edge of the bath.

314 *Scorched irons*

Should the iron get scorched, it can be easily cleaned with aerosol oven cleaner.

315

Keep the bottom of the iron clean by occasionally ironing (cold) over a sheet of very fine sandpaper.

316
Brown stains can be removed from the bottom of the iron with a soap pad.

317 *Furring*
When defrosting the fridge, save the water and use it in your steam iron. This will prevent it from furring up.

318 *Starch*
Half a teaspoonful of salt, added to the starch water, makes things easier to iron.

319 *Starched clothes*
Damp starched clothes with hot water and the iron will glide easily over them.

320 *Using up soap*
To use up the last pieces of white beauty soap, place them on a piece of clean unprinted paper, run a warm iron over this, then over a second sheet of paper to remove any surplus soap. The iron will then glide over garments and give them a lovely smell.

321 *Ironing boards*
Buy an ironing board with adjustable heights and learn to iron sitting down. Never stand to do a chore if you can sit!

Kitchen and household

Bottle marks
322
To eliminate rings caused by containers on cupboard shelves, press a piece of tin foil around the base of each container. This will save a lot of unnecessary cleaning.

Washing powder
323
Make a hole in a detergent packet with a pencil or sharp object instead of opening the flap. This gives greater control over pouring, and is more economical.

Vacuum cleaning
324
When using a vacuum cleaner, put half a fresh air tablet in the dust bag. This leaves a pleasant smell everywhere you clean.

Damp matches
325
Avoid damp matches by placing a bean in each matchbox.

Dry tobacco
326
Tobacco tends to become dry. Avoid this by placing a piece of raw potato in with it. This does not make the tobacco taste, but keeps it moist.

Clean cooking
327
Place a piece of paper kitchen towel roll next to the stove when cooking and stand greasy cooking implements on this.

328
Place used cooking utensils in a jug of soapy water as soon as you have finished with them.

Knife handles
329
A loose knife handle can be fixed with a mixture consisting of

equal quantities of brick dust and resin. Fill the hole in the handle with the mixture, then heat the metal prong of the knife and press it firmly into the handle.

Sealing letters
330
A letter or packet sealed with glue can be steamed open. Sealing with white of egg makes this impossible.

Parcels
331
To tie packages extra securely, wet the string before using. As it dries, it shrinks and so becomes tighter.

Moth balls
332
Hang moth preventatives as high up as possible since the fumes are heavy and filter downwards.

Cartons
333
Save the plastic cartons that honey, cheese, etc. are bought in. Covered with adhesive plastic, they look decorative and are useful for picnics and as storage containers.

Screw-top jars
334
Save instant coffee, or other screw-top jars. Paint the lids with enamel paint, to match the kitchen, and use for storing spices, etc.

335
If you are short of space in your kitchen screw the jar lids to the underside of the larder shelves, and store the jars that way.

Opening bottles
336
Tight screw-topped bottles can often be opened by using a pair of nut crackers.

Or else immerse the top in hot water, which will cause it to expand.

Or wind a wide rubber band around the top to give a good grip.

Or wear a rubber glove to unscrew a stubborn top.

Corkscrews
337
A screw, attached to a piece of string, makes a very good substitute for a corkscrew.

Opening tins
338
A meat skewer threaded through the hole in the key type of tin opener and used to give leverage, helps open stubborn tins.

Dustbins
339
Clean and dry the dustbin then line with newspaper. Never put any wet rubbish in the bin without wrapping it first. Tear or squash all cartons flat. Fill tins with smaller tins or rubbish. Besides condensing the rubbish this will also reduce the number of wasps and flies and make the refuse collector's job less unpleasant.

Gas burners
340
Never light the front burners on the gas stove before the back ones, or your sleeve or blouse may catch alight.

Saucepan lid
341
Many milk saucepans are sold without a much-needed lid. A cheap one can be made from a $1\frac{1}{2}$-lb instant-coffee lid, with a hole punched in the centre and a brightly coloured knob screwed in.

Funnels
342
Half an eggshell makes a neat funnel for filling narrow-necked bottles or cruets. Wash the shell carefully in clean water, allow to dry, then pierce a hole in the end with a darning needle.

Scissors
343
To sharpen blunt scissors, cut them repeatedly on the neck of a glass bottle.

Carving knives
344
Keep your carving knife in an old glove in the kitchen drawer to avoid accidental cuts.

China teapots
345
When putting a china teapot away, wrap a small piece of cloth or bandage round the spout to prevent it getting chipped or broken.

Tea drips
346
To avoid getting tea drips on the tablecloth, cut a ring of foam rubber and fit this over the spout of the teapot.

Household notes
347
Jot down household notes on a glazed tile, using a felt pen. The tile can, of course, be wiped clean time after time.

Kettles
348
A marble in the kettle will prevent it from furring up.

Spiders in the bath
349
Spiders get into the bath via the overflow, not the plug hole. So block the overflow with plasticine to prevent their coming.

Blocked pipes
350
To free a blocked sink or basin, fill an empty washing-up liquid container with water, insert the nozzle in the plughole and fire the water down.

Kitchen curtains

351
Kitchen curtains hanging near a sink unit or cooker can get very splashed and messy. While you work in the kitchen, slot the curtain ends into a polythene bag to keep them clean.

Firelighters

352
Save the skins of oranges and grapefruits and dry them under the grill. When dry, they help start the fire since they are full of oil.

353
Cinders soaked in paraffin make excellent firelighters. Keep a small quantity of paraffin in an old tin and add a few cinders each night. In the morning they will be well soaked and it will be easy to get the fire going.

Smoking chimneys

354
To clear a smoking chimney, put some dry potato peelings, mixed with two handfuls of salt, on the fire when it is glowing red.

Lampshades

355
Before fitting new lampshades to a light fitting, smear the inside grooves of the retaining ring with vaseline, or a similar lubricant, for easier removal when cleaning.

Rugs

356
Fix small pieces of foam rubber to the four corners of a rug and it will not slip on a polished floor.

Clothes lines

357
Clothes lines can be kept clean by having a detachable end at one end of the line and keeping it coiled in a polythene bag hung at the other end.

Egg cosies
358
When outgrown, babies' mittens make good egg cosies.

Ice trays
359
Smear a thin coat of petroleum jelly on the outsides of metal containers placed in the ice box. This will prevent them sticking, and they will pull out without any trouble.

Fizzy drinks
360
To stop the remainder of a fizzy drink going flat, replace the cap and seal with adhesive tape.

Candles
361
To prevent grease running down candles and to prolong their life, coat them with varnish and leave to dry.

362
Candles burn more slowly if kept in a fridge for a few hours before using.

Coal
363
Coal will last longer if sprinkled with a mixture of a tablespoonful of soda to two quarts of water and allowed to dry before using.

Nettles
364
A bunch of fresh stinging nettles hung up at the window will prevent flies coming in.

Quicklime
365
A box of quicklime placed in a damp cupboard will quickly absorb the moisture.

Sellotape
366
When using sellotape, put a small button under the end, as you use it, and you will have no difficulty in finding the end again.

Plastic bags

367

When drying the inside of a plastic bag, put in a dry cloth, screw up the top of the bag and shake it around. The cloth will absorb the moisture.

Clothes sprinkler

368

To make an unbreakable clothes sprinkler, or mini watering can, remove the top from an empty washing-up liquid container and afix a small rose which you can buy from any hardware shop.

Tin foil

369

Line cake storage tins with tin foil. This can be washed and frequently re-used.

Cake tins

370

If a cake tin is unavailable, use a casserole dish or meat tin lined with greased paper.

Toothbrushes

371

A new toothbrush makes easy work of cleaning celery.

An old one is useful for cleaning awkward places on bicycles.

Small kitchens

372

To obtain more working space in a small kitchen, place a laminated board over the sink. This provides an extra surface, and will slide along or lift off when the sink is needed.

Sewing

Odds and ends

373
Pin a paper bag to the wall near the sewing table and put in it all those scraps of cotton and material that would otherwise be dropped on the floor.

374
Put newspaper over the floor before sewing to catch all bits and pieces of thread etc.

Cutting out

375
When cutting out and sewing flimsy materials, try stitching clear sticky tape along the line you are to cut. This prevents the material fraying or slipping.

376
First heat the scissors before cutting nylon. This seals the edges.

377
Paint clear nail varnish along the edge you are going to cut, to prevent fraying.

Short measures

378
Cut three or four inches from an old tape measure and paste onto a piece of belt stiffening. Useful for all short measurements.

Buttons

379
To remove buttons without cutting the cloth, place a comb between the button and material and cut with a pair of scissors or razor blade, between the button and the comb.

Shanks

380
Place a match across the top of a button, sew loosely over it, then remove the match and wind the thread round under the button to make a shank.

381
For smaller buttons on finer cloth use a needle instead of a match.

382
Buy a small piece of plastic, $\frac{1}{8}$ in. thick, 4 in. long and 1 in. wide. Cut a slit 2 in. long and $\frac{1}{16}$ in. wide. Sew the button onto the garment through the slit then remove the plastic. Wind the thread round and fasten it off.

Sewing machines
383
If you find your sewing machine too heavy to lift, keep it permanently on a trolley. It will be at a convenient height and easy to move from place to place.

Darning
384 *Wool*
Always pre-shrink shanks of darning wool in hot water. The darns will not then contract when washed.

385 *Gloves*
A marble, dropped in the finger of a glove, will make a mini-mushroom when darning.

386 *Socks*
Use an old electric light bulb for darning socks.

387 *Changing sleeves*
Change sleeves over from left to right in children's jumpers and cardigans when they show signs of wear. This saves darning.

Worn sheets
388
Make pillow cases from the best part of worn linen sheets.

Old flannelette sheets make excellent drying-up cloths.

Stiff zips
389
To ease stiff zips, rub a soft lead pencil along its teeth – and always wash garments with the zips closed.

Shortening sleeves

390
When shortening sleeves of coats, make a tuck in the lining instead of undoing both the coat and the lining.

Patterns

391
Before making up a 'cut out and ready to sew' garment, take a duplicate of the pattern pieces for future use.

Belts

392
Turn a long narrow belt from each end towards the middle, leaving about four or five inches unsewn in the centre. Then push each end through to the centre with a knitting needle and carefully hand-stitch the remaining few inches.

Cotton reels

393
Thread reels of cotton onto a length of elastic and join together with a safety pin. If a reel is required for sewing, simply push the one needed round to the pin and slip it off.

Padded hangers

394
Save old nylons, wash them, bind them very tightly round ordinary wooden coat hangers, then cover with velvet or silk.

Needles

395
Thread needles over a piece of white card or paper – it makes it much easier.

Darning needles

396
Darning needles can be threaded by threading a loop of 5 amp fuse wire through the eye, put the wool through the loop, then pull the wire and wool back through the needle.

Pockets

397
Pockets lined with chamois leather will last much longer.

Flock nylon

398

Flock nylon, left over from making curtains, can be made into attractive dressing-table mats if you cut round the raised pattern. No sewing is needed.

Mending nets

399

Mend holes in net curtains by arranging the threads together, then coating with clear nail varnish. This will withstand light washing.

Knitting

Smooth hands
400
Dust your hands with talcum powder before you start knitting.
This smooths the hands and prevents snags in the wool.

Casting-on
401
When casting-on wool for children's clothes, to give plenty of
stretch, use a size larger needle than stated in the pattern.

402
When casting-on, put the needle behind the stitch instead of
into it. This makes a firm edge and does away with the need to
knit into the back of the stitch on the first row.

Casting-off
403
When casting-off the neck of a jumper, always use a size larger
needle than the pattern says; this ensures a good stretch.

Increasing
404
When knitting small children's cardigans, knit both sleeves or
fronts on the same needles, using two balls of wool. On larger
garments, thread a piece of contrasting wool through the first
few stitches on each increase row; the rows have then only to
be counted from the last increase. After the piece is finished,
the strands are simply removed by pulling gently.

Joining wool
405
To join wool together simply darn one end into the other for
about three to four inches; the result is a very neat join.

406
Or unravel about three inches from each ball and repeatedly
twist the ends together between index finger and thumb.

Neat finish
407
Pick up the stitches round the neck of a pullover with a double-

ended knitting needle, then knit them off the other end. This gives a neater finish to the garment.

Dark wool
408
If knitting with dark-coloured wool strains your eyes, cover your lap with a white cloth thus making a contrasting background. This is particularly useful if following a lace pattern.

Row counters
409
When accurate row counting is important (such as when knitting socks), thread your row counter on a piece of tape and hang it round your neck. This will prevent you dropping it on the floor.

Cable needles
410
When knitting a cable pattern, use a crochet hook instead of a cable needle; the hook stops stitches sliding off the loops.

411
Use an orange stick instead of a cable needle; it will never fall out of your knitting.

Enough wool
412
To test if there is sufficient wool to complete another row: if you can stretch it across the work three times there is enough.

Button holes
413
To make a strong button hole when knitting: knit three, cast off three, knit three; Second row: knit three, cast on four, knit three; Third row: knit two, knit two together, knit six.

Right size
414
A knitting pattern giving several sizes is simpler to follow if you first underline all the directions in the size you require.

Knitting-needle holders
415
Corrugated cardboard makes an excellent knitting-needle

holder. Insert each needle between a ridge with all the knobs at one end. Roll up the card and secure with a rubber band or piece of ribbon.

Unwanted woollens
416
Unwanted woollen jumpers and cardigans can be cut down for children, providing the cut edges are then crocheted or blanket-stitched.

Ribbing
417
To prevent the ribbed part of a pullover or cardigan from going baggy, knit the plain stitches, put the wool forward, slip the purl stitches and continue in this way.

Cardigans
418
Knit the borders of a cardigan together on a pair of needles to ensure that they are of the same length. The ends can then be grafted together and the cardigan sewn up.

Hairpins
419
When joining parts of knitted garments together, use fine hair-pins instead of dressmakers' pins.

420
Use a hairpin instead of a safety pin for holding small numbers of stitches – the stitches can then be slipped off either end.

Seams
421
Do not sew the seams of knitted or crocheted garments; crochet them together with double crochet, if you should ever want to take the garment apart, you then have only to find the thread at the end of the seam and pull.

Difficult patterns
422
When knitting complicated patterns clip a piece of card below the line worked on. This is easily moved as the work progresses and is useful for jotting down rows worked, repeats, etc.

Do it yourself

Painting
423 *Ceilings*
When emulsioning a ceiling, tie a piece of string across the top of the tin and use it to wipe any surplus paint off the brush.

424 *Straining paint*
Use old nylon stockings for straining paint.

425 *Storing paint*
Before storing an opened tin of gloss paint, float a small quantity of turpentine over the top of the paint before replacing the lid and it will never go hard.

426
Turn a tin of paint upside down when storing and you will never be troubled with a skin on the paint.

Storing brushes
427
After cleaning paint off distemper brushes, bind the bristles with strips of old cloth. This will absorb the moisture, and stop the bristles from curling.

Softening brushes
428
To soften paint brushes, soak them in vinegar heated to just below boiling point.

Paint drips
429
Affix a sponge to the handle of a paint brush when emulsioning ceilings and it will catch paint drips.

430
A paper picnic plate, glued to the bottom of a tin of paint, will catch any drips and provide a stand for the paint brush.

Paint smells

431

When painting, cut an onion in half and place it high up on a shelf or cupboard; it will check the smell of paint.

432

Or try placing half an onion in a bucket of water in the middle of the room. The onion will absorb the smell in a few hours.

Windows

433

Before painting round windows, line the glass close to the frames with sticky tape. Paint as usual then remove the tape – no messy windows.

Wallpaper

434 *Stripping wallpaper*

When stripping washable wallpapers, put the prepared solution on with a pot scourer. This scratches the surface enabling the water to soak through.

435

Use a garden hoe to strip wallpaper high up. This saves having to climb up a ladder.

436

Alum, added to a bucket of water, can be used to remove old wallpaper.

437 *Replacing paper*

When you paper a room, cut some additional lengths of wallpaper and pin them to the back of a wardrobe or cupboard. These will tone with the paper on the walls and should you need to replace a strip, it will match the rest of the room.

Covered tins

438

Large tins, covered with wallpaper, can be used either as wastepaper baskets, or linen baskets, according to size.

Barrels

439

A barrel, cut in half vertically then cleaned and polished and with the hoops firmly screwed on and fitted inside with shelves makes a very attractive bar and will take up hardly any space.

Table mats

440
Should the pictures wear off your table-mats, stick coloured doilies on them and then cover with a coat of varnish.

Deck chairs

441
Before covering a deck chair, wrap felt round the two horizontal bars and the canvas will last longer.

442
When covering deck chairs, use a double length of canvas and fit like a roller towel without nailing. The canvas can then be moved as it wears.

Stiff latch

443
A little vaseline will loosen a stiff door latch.

Screws

444
When using screws for woodwork, first rub them across a bar of soap. This prevents them from rusting, and makes their removal easier.

445
To remove an obstinate screw, first heat the screwdriver.

Drilling

446
When drilling thick metal, make good use of your centre punch and deep punch the metal frequently. This helps to make the drill point 'bite' and cuts down effort. A few spots of oil on the drill will help by keeping the drill cool. This applies to hand or electric drills.

Gardening

Ants
447
If you are pestered with ants coming into the house, draw a thick boundary line with children's chalk and you will find that the ants will not cross this.

448
Powdered borax, sprinkled around ants' nest, will soon kill them.

Slugs
449
To keep slugs away from plants, collect eggshells, then bake them in a warm oven to harden the shells. Crush and scatter them round the plant stems and the slugs will be unable to climb over the shells.

450
Slugs can be killed by sprinkling them with salt.

Privet flowers
451
Pick all flowers, within children's reach, off privet hedges as they turn to poisonous berries.

Tomatoes
452
Grow your tomatoes in cheap plastic buckets. Cut out the bottom of the bucket with a sharp knife, leaving a lip (warming the knife will make cutting easier). You will be able to use these year after year, and have a very colourful greenhouse too.

Roses
453
Add a little cold water to leftover tea and use this to water the roses.

Manure

454

Fill an old bucket or tank with freshly mown grass cuttings; fill this up with water and leave to ferment; the result is a very fine liquid manure.

Fertiliser

455

Half fill a jar with eggshells, fill up with water and leave to stand for three weeks. It makes a good fertiliser for plants.

Small seeds

456

Before sowing small seeds, mix them with sand. Water the drills well then sprinkle the mixture in. There is no need to cover with soil.

Planting peas or beans

457

Soak newspapers or old cushions in water overnight, put all the soaked material in the bottom of the trench, add a small layer of earth, then scatter in the peas or beans and cover with earth.

Gardening bands

458

When rubber gloves are worn out, cut off the cuffs and cut them into various widths of rubber bands. Very useful for tying up plants – especially daffodils in the spring.

459

Old stockings, cut into rings, are very useful for tying up plants.

Daffodils

460

Instead of waiting until daffodils and narcissi grow tall and need staking, stick some twigs criss-cross fashion over the ground where the bulbs are planted. The flowers will not need staking, and will not grow all bunched together.

Fallen leaves

461

Lay a large tarpaulin or thick curtain on the ground, then sweep all the fallen leaves into it. Pick up the four corners and pile the leaves on a compost heap.

Pruning roses
462
When pruning brambled roses, or any other prickly plants, put all the cuttings on an old sack or thick curtain, then you can dispose of the cuttings scratch-free.

Geraniums
463
Leave geraniums in their pots when planted in the flower beds, then they can easily be taken indoors for the winter.

Butterflies
464
To attract butterflies to your garden, plant a buddleia shrub.

Garden kneelers
465
An old rubber hot-water bottle will make a splendid garden kneeler if you cut off the top and stuff the bottle with shredded nylon stockings. It is waterproof and easily cleaned.

466
Make a garden kneeling-cushion using plastic on one side, material on the other and discarded nylons as stuffing. The plastic being waterproof goes on the ground and the material side is comfortable.

Stakes
467
The handle of an old birch broom makes a good strong stake; broken twigs are useful for propping up small plants.

Raking
468
Raking leaves is made much easier if a strip of stiff yet flexible material, like rubber-backed underfelt, is threaded in and out of the teeth of the rake. The strip should be one inch longer than the width of the teeth and secured at each end with wire.

Cut flowers and houseplants

Plant pots

469

Save plastic food containers, take three, cut the bottoms out of two, coat them with white glue, place them inside the whole one, and you have a plant pot for indoor flowers. Decorate with transfers or pictures from magazines or old greetings cards.

Cut flowers

470 *Stagnant smells*

A few drops of household bleach, added to the water of cut flowers, prevents the water from going stale and does not harm the flowers.

471

A teaspoonful of sugar plus a teaspoonful of bleach will stop flower water from smelling.

472

Stagnant smells from cut flowers can be avoided if you place a piece of charcoal in the bottom of the vase of water.

Cut flowers

473

Cut flowers will last much longer if arranged in cold tea.

Tulips

474

When tulips start to wilt, pierce the stem about a quarter-of-an-inch below the flower head, and they will quickly revive.

Chrysanthemums

475

Should chrysanthemums start to wilt, dip the stems in boiling water for a couple of minutes and then into cold water.

Short stems

476

If the stems of flowers are too short for the chosen vase, screw up some newspaper and put this at the bottom. Fill with water and rest the stems on the paper – it also helps hold the flowers in position.

Leaky vase

477

A tumbler or jar placed inside a leaky vase will hold the water and be inconspicuous.

Children

Watching trees
478
Place baby's pram under a tall tree and he will spend hours watching the branches move.

Safety nets
479
A safety net over a pram keeps a baby occupied trying to grasp the net – as well as keeping cats off!

Carrycots
480
Put the carrycot handles inside the cot so that the baby can play with them. Soft toys or rattles can be attached to the handles too.

Sleep check
481
Babies can be watched sleeping without being disturbed if you hold a hand mirror at the door of their bedrooms and then turn it until it gives a good view.

Photographs
482
To make your baby sit well when having his photograph taken, stick a small piece of sticky tape on one of his fingers. He will try to remove it and pull lots of faces.

Rubber pants
483
When rubber part of baby's waterproof pants has perished, cut the remains of the plastic away, save the nylon overlay and use to put over plain pants.

Baby's plate
484
Secure baby's food plate to the high chair table with a double-sided suction grip.

Bath toys
485
To keep bath toys tidy, hang them in a string shopping bag over the bath. The toys will then drain into the bath.

Bandages
486
If your children's hands never seem to be without bandages, cover the dressing with a polythene bag before putting on coats and cardigans. Then remove the bag carefully.

487
Cut the feet off children's worn-out socks and use the leg part to cover bandages on legs and arms.

Making candle holders
488
Children can be occupied during illness or on holidays by making decorative candle holders. You will need: tin lids or bottle tops; a packet of plaster filler; coloured candles; gold and silver lacquer paint, glitter, small leaves, fircones, dried beach-nut cases etc. Put a small lump of plaster in the centre of a tin lid, press the candle in to make the holder shape, remove candle, then decorate the plaster while it's wet, or else glue the decorations to it when dry.

Travel sickness
489
Give children a boiled sweet to suck on car journeys; it helps to avoid travel sickness.

Seaside
490
Save the containers that fancy mousses are sold in. They can be used by children to make sandpies with, by the sea.

491
When drying children after sea bathing, just dab off the water, then powder with baby powder – then drying is not painful.

Bedwetting
492
A plea from a landlady: when taking small children on holiday to a guesthouse, if they are prone to wet the bed please tell your landlady when you arrive so that she can protect the bed.

Polythene bags
493
If you save polythene bags, tie a knot in the centre of the bags. This will prevent children from putting them over their heads.

Pinboard
494
Polystyrene ceiling tiles, fixed to the wall of a teenager's room, make a good pinboard.

Cold hands
495
To protect children's hands when they are playing in the snow, tie small polythene bags over the gloves round the wrists.

Elastic loops
496
When sewing hanging loops in children's clothes, use elastic; the linings are less likely to tear when pulled off the pegs.

497
Stitch a long length of elastic to children's mittens or gloves, long enough to go through the sleeves and coat. This way the gloves will not get lost.

Handkerchiefs
498
Discarded muslin napkins, cut into four and stitched round, make excellent handkerchiefs for school beginners.

Old toothbrushes
499
Use old toothbrushes for cleaning small children's shoes.

Wellington boots
500
Give schoolchildren a peg with their name inked on, to clip their Wellingtons together.

Car hints

Parking
501
Watching your car's reflection in shop windows when parking, can often help in getting into small parking places.

Red triangle
502
Always carry a red triangle in the car in case of breakdown or accident – as they do on the continent.

Car mats
503
Cover the carpet in your car with matching mats. These can be easily removed for cleaning, and can be replaced when threadbare.

Wheel gloves
504
A wheel glove prevents the steering wheel from becoming too hot to handle after being parked in the sun all day.

Leathercloth roofs
505
To retain the good appearance of leathercloth roofs and rubber mats in your car, polish them with shoe polish.

Car doors
506
If your car door is likely to scrape against the wall of your garage, nail a piece of carpet to the wall.

507
The above hint inspired another listener to write:
> No nailed carpet in the garage is needed
> To protect your car door when opened unheeded.
> Fixed with contact adhesive, some foam rubber strip
> Gives ample protection – it's a jolly good tip!

Batteries

508

Save the water while defrosting the fridge, store it in an air-tight glass bottle and use it to top up the car battery.

Winter hazards

509

During winter keep two sacks, with a length of string tied to each, in the car boot. If stuck in the snow or ice, tie the string to the rear doors, place the sacks under the rear wheels and drive clear – you hope! Then untie the sacks.

First aid

Medicines
510
After buying medicine or tablets always write the date of purchase on the bottle or box. You will then know how long you have had the medicine and whether it is still safe to take if needed at a later date.

Daily dosage
511
If you find it difficult to remember whether or not you have taken your tablets, put the daily dosage into a separate box or bottle each day. This does away with the possibility of exceeding the dose.

Sick-room freshener
512
A way of freshening air in a sick room, if aerosol sprays are unacceptable, is to burn a little eau-de-Cologne in a fireproof dish.

Asthma
513
To help relieve asthma, take a teaspoonful of honeycomb each day. (These are obtainable at health-food stores.)

Scalds
514
To relieve pain from a scald, sprinkle flour on the affected area.

515
White of egg, poured over a burn or scald, prevents inflammation and relieves the pain.

Hiccups
516
Try sucking a cube of sugar slowly to cure hiccups.

517
If you have an attack of hiccups, swallow a teaspoonful of vinegar for an almost certain cure.

Aching feet

518

To relieve aching feet, try standing on your toes, several times, and stretching your ankles.

Colds

519

Boiled onions are a good cure for the common cold.

Chilblains

520

If you suffer from chilblains, keep your feet and hands warm and do not wear restricting clothing.

521

To relieve itching chilblains rub them lightly with a piece of raw onion.

Insect repellant

522

If you are troubled by mosquitoes or other insects, buy some oil of citronella and rub it on your face, hands and legs.

Wasp stings

523

Rub wasp stings with a piece of raw onion.

524

If stung by a wasp, suck the spot immediately (if you can). This will diminish the pain and in some cases will remove the sting completely.

Nettle stings

525

Dab nettle stings with vinegar for quick relief.

Splinters

526

A pumice stone, dipped in water and rubbed lightly on the skin, will remove surface splinters without the use of a needle.

527

When removing a splinter from under the nail, cut a 'V' shape in the nail on either side of the splinter. You then should be able to take the splinter out easily.

Miscellaneous

Fastening zips
528
To fasten a long zip at the back of a dress, thread a piece of string with a knot at one end through the eyelet of the zip and pull this up.

Hot-water bottle covers
529
Cut the legs off old pyjama trousers and make them into hot-water bottle covers.

Soft toys
530
Wash and cut up old stockings and tights. They make good stuffing for cushions, or soft toys, and they wash easily.

Cuff-links
531
Join decorative buttons together with strong thread to make unusual cuff-links.

Pets
532 *Giving medicines*
Use a medicine dropper for giving cats and other small animals liquid medicines.

533 *New puppies*
To keep a new puppy or kitten quiet at night, put a loud ticking clock in the bottom of its box or basket together with a warm hot-water bottle and cover with a blanket.

534
A washing-up bowl makes an excellent bed for a new kitten or puppy.

Dandruff

535

A lump of margarine (not butter) fed to a dog suffering from dandruff or dry skin will help to condition its coat.

Beauty

536 *Eyeliner*

Before applying pencil eyeliner, smooth a little petroleum jelly along the lid; the eyeliner can then be applied smoothly and evenly. Set with a dab of face powder.

537 *Brittle nails*

Brittle finger nails can be strengthened by eating a square of table jelly every day and by massaging a little petroleum jelly into the base of the nail each night.

538 *Nail varnish*

If nail varnish gets too hard, thin it down with a little nail varnish remover.

539

To set nail varnish, run your fingers under the cold tap immediately the varnish has dried.

540 *Rough hands*

To smooth roughened hands, roll and knead a small piece of dry bread over them for a few minutes.

541 *Dry shampoo*

Powdered starch makes a good dry shampoo, provided it is brushed out thoroughly.

542 *Dry hands*

If you have dry rough hands, try pouring a little olive oil into the cupped palm, add a little salt, then massage this well into the hands. Leave it on for five minutes, then rinse off with warm water and soap.

Trading stamps

543

Trading stamps can be stuck easily and cleanly into their books by pressing them onto a damp sponge or nail brush.

Addressing envelopes
544
Always write your own address on the back of envelopes. This enables the GPO (now the GPC) to return letters unopened should they be wrongly addressed, or if the person has moved.

Pictures
545
To keep pictures hanging straight, stick on a small piece of foam rubber on the bottom edge of the frame.

Making vases
546
Cut the top off an empty plastic washing-up liquid container, cover the container with liquid plastic, then press shells, pebbles and pieces of coloured glass into this before it hardens.

Shopping list
547
If you are always losing your shopping list, jot down items required on a luggage lable and tie this to the handle of your shopping basket.

Storing onions
548
Store onions in a nylon stocking; tie a knot between each onion, then cut them as required.

Lavender bag
549
Lavender, kept in a stocking hung over the wardrobe rail, gives off a pleasant smell each time the door is opened.

Banking fires
550
When banking up the fire with small coal put a folded damp newspaper on first before adding the coal. This will keep the fire in for a long time and it will burn much cleaner.

Hard glue
551
Add a few drops of vinegar to hard glue and it will soften it up.

Electric blankets

552

When it is time to put the electric blanket on the bed, sew some curtain rings onto the side of the mattress opposite the fixing holes on the blanket, then you only need short ties whichever way up you have your mattress.

Insects

553 *Wasps*

The easiest way of removing a wasp, or other stinging insect, from a car is to cover all windows from the outside with rugs or coats and to leave one door open. Insects always fly towards the light.

554

To catch wasps or bees when they come indoors, open an empty match box about one third and place this over the insect. Shut the box, carry it outside and then release the insect.

555

Exterminate a wasps' nest in the ground by waiting until dusk, when all wasps will be in the nest, then pour a bottle of paraffin into the entrance of the nest. The fumes will asphyxiate the wasps.

556 *Spiders*

To remove spiders from the house without killing them, cover them with a glass tumbler, slide a thin piece of card underneath, take this into the garden and then free the insect.

Doors and windows

557

If doors or windows stick during damp weather, try rubbing all round the edges of the frames with wax floor polish. Rub this well into the woodwork, then polish off; the doors or windows should then glide freely.

Woodworm holes

558

To hide woodworm holes in furniture, fill them with shoe polish which matches the colour of the wood.

Ironing board covers
559
Do not throw away your husband's worn-out pyjama trousers.
Cut off the leg part and slip this over the ironing board; it will
make a marvellous cover.

Razor blades
560
To prolong the use of razor blades, rinse the razor completely
including the blade, shake off the excess moisture and keep the
head of the razor covered with surgical spirit. Besides prevent-
ing rust, this also sterilises the blade.

Shaving cuts
561
Place a small piece of unprinted newspaper over a shaving cut.
The blood then congeals quickly and the paper can be gently
removed.

Sticking furniture
562
Wax polish, candle grease and pencil lead, are some of the sug-
gestions for treating drawers that stick. The drawers should be
taken out and the top, bottom, and runners rubbed well with
the substance.

Pouring paraffin
563
Fit a rubber nozzle to a paraffin can; this makes it easier to
regulate the flow.

50p coin
564
If you use a combined wallet and purse and have no place for
the 50p coin, try sticking a zip in the 10s. note slot with strong
glue.

Notes for tradesmen
565
Notes for tradesmen, kept in an old photo frame hung on the
outside wall, will not get wet, or blow away.

Luggage
566
Cut large initial letters from adhesive material and stick these onto your luggage, which can then be easily identified when you arrive at airport or railway terminals.

Plant pot holders
567
Old bicycle clips make excellent plant pot holders. Drill a hole at the centre of the clip; screw the clip to the wall, then fit the plant pot in.

Picnic cloth
568
Curtain rings sewn to the four corners of a picnic tablecloth enable it to be pegged down in the wind.

Christmas
569 *Baubles*
Looped rubber bands are the best way of fixing baubles to a Christmas tree.

570 *Royal icing*
A few drops of glycerine in royal icing prevents it from going brittle.

571 *Gift tags*
Cut out small pictures from old Christmas or birthday cards and use as gift tags.

572 *Wrapping paper*
Wrapping paper can be re-used if it is first pressed under a dry cloth with a cool iron to remove the creases.

573 *Christmas streamers*
To make a Christmas streamer, get a piece of coloured paper about 3 ft by 6 in. Make a centre crease lengthways and fold outer edges to the centre crease. Fold the strip in half again. Make long diagonal cuts alternately along both sides. Then carefully open out the streamer.

574 *Roses*

To keep roses for Christmas, cut the stems as long as possible, strip off all leaves, seal the stems with candle-grease, and pack the roses in a lightly sealed container taking care not to bruise them. One week before Christmas, take them out of the box, stand them in hand-hot water for two hours to melt the grease, then arrange.

575 *Christmas trees*

To prevent needles falling from Christmas trees, place the trunk in a strong plastic bag half-filled with neat glycerine, seal the bag with an elastic band around the top, then stand the tree in a pot, taking care not to burst the bag.

576 *Table centre*

Collect some small sprigs of twigs (apple is very suitable). Coat them with silver paint. Bore holes in a cake board to fit the twig stems, and arrange these. Finish by hanging with small coloured baubles.

577 *Holly ball*

Thread a length of coloured twine or ribbon, knotted at one end, through the centre of a large potato (choose one of regular shape that will keep an even balance when hanging). Stick spikes of holly into the potato, then hang your holly ball where you will.

578 *Christmas cards*

Make a list of friends that you send cards to, and record presents given, and save these lists from year to year. You will then know how many cards to buy each year and you will never duplicate presents.

Shoes

579 *Wet boots*

To dry out wet boots or shoes, fill them with oats. The oats absorb the moisture and expand slightly and so prevent shoes from shrinking. Shoes should never be dried in front of the fire as this hardens and cracks the leather and mis-shapes the shoes. The oats, once dried, can be used over and over again for this purpose.

580 *Snow shoes*
Before going out in the snow, rub a little fat round the welt and on the sole of the shoe. This stops the snow clinging and makes walking easier.

581 *Suede shoes*
To renovate suede shoes, hold them over steam. Let shoes dry, then brush with suede brush.

582 *Summer shoes*
If you would like to wear shoes without stockings but cannot because they rub, cut out the feet from an old pair of stockings and wear these inside your shoes.

583 *Sling-back shoes*
A very thin strip of adhesive foam draught excluder, stuck to the back of sling-back shoes, will prevent the strap from slipping down.

Toothpaste
584
The last bit of toothpaste can be squeezed from the tube with a rolling pin.

Empty boxes
585
Before throwing empty boxes away, soak them in water for a few seconds. They will then fold very small and take up less space in the dustbin.

Signing cheques
586
Place a piece of thick paper or card underneath a cheque or pension form to keep the impression of your signature from showing on the form below.

Parcels
587
After addressing parcels, lightly rub the address with a candle. This stops rain from smudging the ink.